My Book of PR Tips

Share Your Story with the Media

Linda Reed-Enever

To Clive and Miss C,
who are behind me in all that I do!
Without either of you this journey of life
would not be the same.

Contents

Let's start your PR Journey

Welcome to my book of PR Tips!

This book has been created for and inspired by business owners who want to share their story with the media.

Those who know me know that my little black book has always been red, and now it is time for me to open my Little Red Book and share my PR Tips with you.

My Book of PR Tips has been created as a tool to be added to your PR and Marketing toolkit. And through the book I look forward to joining you on your PR Journey

Thank you to the amazing businesses and people I work with for encouraging me and inspiring me to create this book.

The tips inside are short and sweet allowing you to get the information you need from the book when you need it.

And when you secure a media win do let me know!

As you make your way through the book there will be a number of exercises along the way. So before we get too far in let's stop for a minute and write down some PR Goals you may have.

My PR Goals

_____

_____

_____

_____

_____

_____

_____

_____

_____

_____

_____

_____

_____

_____

_____

_____

CHAPTER ONE

An Introduction to The Media

What is the Media?

Traditional media is print, TV and radio; from your daily news to your monthly magazines and news features.

The digital era has seen the media grow, diversify and morph into the online world. Online media means that the news is now more social. The reach is wider and your audience is more accessible than ever.

Digital media includes blogs, social media channels such as Facebook, online magazines, and online communities. The result is a world of opportunity for business to share their message across a diverse range of platforms in a variety of styles.

In the end, no matter the channel, the media is all about telling stories and communicating. And if you don't share your story, who will?

Industry Terms Explained

Before we start delving into the world of sharing your story with the media, here are some industry terms explained.

It is better to get it right the first time than miss the deadline because you did not want to lose face.

If there is ever a term you need explained when working with the media - ask.

Advertorial: An advertorial is a paid advertisement designed to look like editorial content, while at the same time offering valid information to your prospective clients.

Bio: A bio is a snappy document that outlines an interviewee's area of expertise and experience.

The Brief: Is the set of requirements and instructions of the client for the PR campaign. Journalists often work to a brief from their editors too.

Bulletin: A bulletin is a package of short news summaries on broadcast radio or television.

Captions: Short pieces of text used to denote who is in a picture and what is happening. For newspapers, captions naming people work from left to right. When writing a caption ensure you include the first and last names (not nicknames) of all people in the photo.

Copy: Is the main text of a story, article or web page, etc. You may be asked to submit or review copy over your PR journey.

Cross/ live cross: When a journalist or talent is interviewed in real time at a location away from the studio it is called a cross. When that interview is live to air, it is called a live cross.

Editorial: Editorial features are the articles generated and produced by journalists or freelancers commissioned by the media outlet's editors. There is no advertiser influence in the creation of editorial features.

Five Ws and H: These are the primary questions answered at the outset of a release and news story:

Who? What? When? Where? Why? And then How?

Format: Format indicates the specifications for an item submitted to the media. It generally applies to image, video and audio files. For example, you might be requested to submit images in JPEG format at a resolution of 1920 x 760. Pay attention to the formats used or any specifications set. These will determine whether an item can be used or not.

Grabs: Are very short sequences/footage (7-10 seconds) that enable the audience to hear/see the news directly from the people involved.

Intro/Outro: Are the opening and closing sequences of a story.

Layout: The format of a print publication or web page determined by advertising placement and style. The volume of advertising for a publication affects the page count, the space a journalist will write to for a story, the size of a photograph and how much a sub-editor will cut in order to fit a story in.

Lead: The first paragraph of a news story or the item that "leads" a bulletin.

LVO: In television media, LVO stands for long voice over where a story is told by the newsreader to accompanying images. It is shorter than a traditional package.

News angle: The "angle" of a story is the particular focus of the story (e.g. the threat to public safety of a chemical spill).

News event: A news event is something newsworthy that happens, e.g. terrorist attack, disaster, major crime etc.

Package: In broadcast media a package is a completed news story with voice and images. Newsreaders introduce the item and then "throw to" the package.

Piece to camera: When the reporter speaks to the camera as part of a television news story.

Rundown: The order in which stories are placed within a bulletin or publication.

Sub-edit or sub: The process prior to publication where copy is edited, formatted and laid out while checking for inaccuracies and style.

Standfirst: In print publications, the standfirst is a brief summary of an article in a newspaper or on a website. It typically appears immediately after the headline and is typographically distinct from the rest of the article.

Style Guide: The Style Guide is a publication's in-house guide for journalists/employees to use and includes details of the style of grammar, spelling, capitalisation etc.

It is very important that you follow the style guide when you submit your articles and releases.

Talent: A person interviewed for a story.

Target audience: Is just like the target audience in business. It is the specific group the particular media outlet/entity appeals to.

Voice over: A voice over in radio or television is the verbal telling of the story that accompanies images and audio.

_____

_____

_____

_____

_____

_____

_____

_____

_____

_____

_____

_____

_____

CHAPTER TWO

What is PR?

Public Relations is all about relating your business to the public: telling your story, building your brand and sharing your message in a way that the media and general population will relate to you, bond with you, and recognise your brand.

Every business, brand and corporation has a story to tell – an idea or ethos that is unique to them. It is this story that the media want to hear.

At its heart, public relations is about telling that story over and over again in a number of ways.

Great public relations is about telling that story well, at the right time, with the right focus and feel, to the right audience.

PR is mostly a proactive world, but occasionally it's reactive. It is a matter of thinking on your feet and being able to do both, to ensure you seize and make the most of opportunities.

Many businesses and organisations often underestimate the power and range of public relations, confining it to media releases. It is much more than that, PR is relationships and it is in those relationships that the power is held.

In this digital age, the world of PR has expanded and, in addition to media marketing and advertising, its realm now encompasses social media, blogging and more.

PR connects a business with its public and provides them the information they need to make decisions about the feel of the business and about its products.

PR Takes Time

Public relations and marketing take time. You cannot work on PR one day and forget about it the next.

Public relations and branding involve a continual process that becomes part of the way you do business and how you shape your day. It is this time commitment by yourself or a professional that makes PR really work for you.

The Three Frontiers of PR

Public relations can be broadly broken down into three primary frontiers that every business should be utilising: proactive, reactive, and ongoing.

In a bid to maximise your PR investment we'll be addressing all throughout this book. So, let's take a quick look at the differences so you can implement them into your day.

Proactive PR is about getting your message out, and it happens in a number of ways including announcing new products, initiatives, an award, a high-profile new staff member or event.

It's usually defined as something that happens within your business that you would like to share with the world.

Reactive PR

Reactive PR occurs in response to something, be it an announcement by another party, a discussion you can contribute to or in rare cases, handling a negative situation.

While it's nature may be reactive, business can use it to great effect by actively seeking out opportunities to respond.

For example, you're a pool fencing business. The government introduces new fencing laws. You respond with a release welcoming the changes and providing homeowners with six essential tips to bring their fences up to par.

A further example is the Federal Budget. Each year the government announces rafts of funding outlays and cuts. If they relate to your industry, your business comes out welcoming or "slamming" the changes.

Ongoing PR

Often underutilised, ongoing PR provides an opportunity to share information with the media at any time.

Using tools such as evergreen content that we'll discuss at length later, ongoing PR extends to tips, advice and utilising common events like Valentine's Day, Christmas or Easter.

This is the PR that never goes out of style, and you find it everywhere from newspapers and magazines to websites and business blogs.

The Platforms of PR

Where once the media was restricted to print, TV and radio, now it extends beyond into the online realm.

That opens up a wealth of opportunities when it comes to getting a message out, but also calls for different strategies to reach an audience. Here's a quick rundown on the various platforms of PR and how they can be utilised to tell your story.

Traditional Media

When we think of the media the mind inevitably turns to TV, Print and Radio. These traditional platforms still represent some of the best mediums for relating your message to the widest audience.

Usually handled by professional journalists and working on the newsroom system, the traditional media are targeted by media releases and interact via interview or event coverage.

Online Media

Online media is becoming an increasingly valuable tool for businesses keen to spread their message. With an endless realm of specialist and niche websites, it widens the opportunity for media exposure. Online media to consider includes:

- Traditional media using websites to tell more stories than their pages or bulletins will permit.

- News sites without a physical presence like Buzzfeed or the Huffington Post.

- Industry sites that relate the latest news specifically pertinent to their membership.

- Topical sites like parenting blogs that share contributor articles, paid posts, and commissioned articles relating to their niche.

- Podcasts.

- Online TV channels.

- Social Media channels.

These are targeted either by media release or article submission.

_____

_____

_____

_____

_____

_____

_____

_____

_____

_____

_____

CHAPTER THREE

Creating a Media Strategy

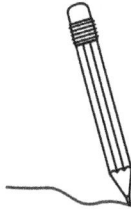

There is no *one size fits all* when it comes to creating the right PR strategy for a business.

The trick is to know where your audience is likely to be and make the most of the opportunity that the media gives you by doing the following:

Plan, Plan, Plan!

Before you look to engage with the media do some planning.

Ask yourself, what are the critical messages that you want to communicate? Your key messages are the core items you want your audience to hear and remember about you and your business.

Have a great bio

PR starts with a great bio that sells you. Your bio should:

- Say who you are
- Tell the reader what you do
- Establish expertise and credibility
- Qualify your experience and background

Remember to include your social media links and website.

Make it easy for the media to connect with you.

Be on the lookout

Those with the best media presence are always on the lookout for opportunity, and it's imperative to know where yours may arise.

Opportunity doesn't just present itself in the form of a journalist who comes knocking to tell your tale.

It happens daily, weekly and monthly in all sorts of places - the government announcement that relates to your industry, the advice you could offer on an industry website, or the timely tips you could share with a magazine that show your authority in your realm.

This involves being across the issues, areas and relevant media for your industry, through media monitoring, research or even Google alerts to know where and when discussion is likely to occur.

We'll delve more into spotting opportunity throughout this book, but at its basis the question is:

"Do I have something to talk about? Can I add to this discussion?"

PR Planning Tips

Keep a notepad handy - A great PR idea may arrive when your phone battery is dead, or you're standing in a supermarket queue, so jot things down as they come to you.

Create a contact list - Start creating a contact list of media professionals and outlets pertinent to your industry.

Create a spreadsheet of release ideas - Go through your business calendar and note dates, events or occasions that may warrant a media release, and put them into a spreadsheet.

Create an article bank - Once you know where your audience is and the outlets that relate to them, you can start creating an article bank of evergreen content to roll out as part of your strategy.

Check twice - When you do send something to the media or submit an article to a website **get someone to read over your work before you send it.**

You know your story well and can often overlook mistakes in your articles and releases.

You know what it is meant to say, so can miss the little things.

Don't give up! - If your initial pitch didn't work, don't take it personally or let it stop you. These things take time.

Let the media get to know you - Journalists are working to a number of different deadlines and demands, which can all change in an instant.

If your story does not run – try a different angle. Don't give up!

There's no such thing as free PR

There is often a misconception that PR just happens, that it's free and easy to come by. The truth is all public relations requires an investment.

That story about the up and coming entrepreneur you read in yesterday's paper, that blog on your favourite website that piqued your interest or that social media campaign that saw emails delivered directly to your inbox all took an investment of time, resources and in some cases paid writing.

Behind every PR campaign there's a host of legwork, and a concerted effort to get the message out. PR takes persistence, knowledge, energy and commitment. Whether you outsource your PR or do it in house, these factors have value.

The ultimate cost - Time

Above all, creating a media presence takes time. Like a concert, the end result may be seamless singing and choreographed staging, but for the two hours the audience sees, there's months of work behind the scenes.

Any business looking to attract media attention needs the strategy and dedication to do it, and to be seen at the right place in the right way.

That means taking the time to:

Create profiles and bios for yourself and your business: From LinkedIn to Facebook pages and websites, complete profiles of an individual or organisation help them to be seen. These details fill in the gaps for the media but also create a "standing" where your presence is established and complete.

Craft newsworthy releases: Good press releases that are likely to attract attention boast a number of ingredients, whether they highlight something new, respond to something timely, or promote an event.

This means they need to be researched and crafted correctly, in the best format to catch an editor's eye.

Find journalists: Not all media outlets and journalists are the same. Certain journalists specialise in specific fields and different media, and make no mistake it takes time and effort to find the right person to pitch to in the right way.

Is it hard news, a feature piece, real estate, lifestyle or health? Not only do you need to have an idea of where you want your story to be seen but know the name of the person or department that will be likely to write it.

Pitch your story: So you've found your target demographic. You know the media outlet most likely to run your story and even the name of the journalist you want to contact. Now it's time for the pitch.

Pitching should be outlet specific addressing what's in it for their audience. And it's not just a matter of whipping up a release and emailing it through.

Pitching often involves a follow-up call to ensure your information has reached the right contact, and to see if there is any interest.

Respond to callouts: Yes, occasionally the media comes a-calling, seeking out stories and themes. But there's no one-size fits all response, and this means thought and effort is required.

It also takes time to be across callouts and to vary your pitch to suit a media outlet's angle.

_____

_____

_____

_____

_____

_____

_____

_____

_____

_____

CHAPTER FOUR

Know Your Media

While the high-profile mainstream media of TV, radio and print are probably the favoured candidates on your PR hit list, you also need to think outside this realm to build your profile.

This involves understanding all the places where your audience seeks their news and being aware of what's being covered, when.

By knowing your media you create more potential venues to:

- Join discussion via reactive PR
- Target your audience with proactive stories pertinent to them
- Provide ongoing publicity through evergreen content

There are a host of ways to find your media, including:

Google alerts: Yes, it is that simple! Set up an alert using keywords related to your industry or people within it, and be informed when and where news pops up.

Media monitoring: There is a variety of paid services dedicated to monitoring news content about every industry, delivering analysis and feeds straight to you that can tell you what's being said within your realm or even what's being said about you.

News distribution services: Another great tool is media distribution services.

These not only provide a platform for journalists calling out to people for stories and interviews in your field, but are also a means to send your media release, article or idea directly to the media that covers your industry.

Once you know where your audience is looking and who's saying what, when, you can build your credibility by writing articles for publications and submitting releases directly to where your market is.

This is the basis of your all-important media contact list and your media strategy.

What the media seeks

Each day, hundreds of media releases pour into metropolitan and regional news outlets across the country, with editors taking only a moment to decide what makes the grade and what hits the cutting room floor.

That means your media release has only a fraction of a second to pique their interest and inspire further investigation. So, what are they looking for and how do you gain their attention?

New

New developments, innovations or programs that solve real problems are among the stories news outlets may look at, depending on the day or week and what else is going on in their demographic.

If this new development applies to a wide section of their audience, that's also going to help. This is why stories about medical developments in the field of cancer tend to make the news; it directly affects so many people and indirectly impacts many more.

Timely

Often there are major issues or important dates that crop up during the year and if a company or body responds to them in a timely manner via reactive PR, they're more likely to get a run.

Take for example "schoolies week". Come November, news outlets will be actively seeking schoolies related stories including tips on sending your teen to schoolies and ways to stay safe.

This also applies to government announcements that may affect an organisation. If something happens to impact business or groups the best time to respond is immediately...as in that day, not the next or a few days later.

Human Interest

There is always a section of news production dedicated to human interest – the hometown girl who now heads up the Commonwealth Bank, the grandmother who knitted 1000 socks for the baby ward at the hospital.

If you have a fascinating story to tell about your business or staff members then use it, targeting it at the media outlet/s most suitable.

Clarity

A media release should be clear, free from jargon and include the who, what, when, where and why in the introduction. Chances are an editor or chief of staff will make their decision based on the first few lines of any release.

And remember, if they seek to run the release in its original form, they will ALWAYS cut from the bottom up.

Headlines

The headline is the first clue as to why your story may interest them, so keep it short, snappy but informative.

The likelihood is they may not use the headline you provide, but your job is to get them to read it.

Consider: "New website to save households hundreds on power bills" or "Body corporate representative slams government reform".

Audience

Each type of news outlet has a different audience, so target them accordingly.

The nightly TV news is unlikely to run a story about your employee who won six industry awards at a national level, but the local newspaper could.

What's in it for Them?

If you're promoting an event or launch, indicate to the news outlet who will be available to speak with them, any extra "talent" or celebrities you may have at hand, and the type of pictures they may get.

Not Advertising

If it feels like your business is seeking free advertising, news outlets will run a mile.

That's what advertorials and paid promotions are for.

So give them what they want, something newsworthy, fresh or human interest, and don't expect them to plug your product for you.

Make it Easy

Always provide further information as to who the news outlet should contact or interview.

If your issue is complex or your product has a background, include a further attachment for their background information, but do not get bogged down in wordy explanations within your release.

Short and Sweet

A media release should be no longer than one A4 page, that's about 400-500 words plus a headline and contact information.

Are you Media Ready?

Before you put pen to paper to draft an article or whip up a release, have you:

- ✓ Honed the key messages your company wants to deliver?
- ✓ Researched where news about your industry is being relayed via a Google news search?
- ✓ Created a list of sites and outlets relevant to you?
- ✓ Set up Google alerts of news pertaining to your industry?
- ✓ Made a shortlist of places you may like to target?
- ✓ Noted down relevant journalists specialising in your industry?
- ✓ Googled your own company to know what is being said about you?

Created a boilerplate and template for your releases?

_____

_____

_____

_____

_____

_____

_____

_____

CHAPTER FIVE

Becoming a Credible Source

A key ingredient to gaining media attention is simply being a credible source. This basically means the media comes to know and trust you as someone reliable who makes producing a good story easy.

Becoming this trusted 'talent' takes time, but it always starts with the basics including being clear on who you are, what you offer, and providing accurate information the media can readily access and check.

So, let's step through the art of being a good source.

The Credibility Factor

Whether you go to the media with a story idea or they come to you seeking someone to comment on a story, the key factor every media professional seeks in a source is credibility.

Credibility encompasses a wealth of factors including your standing in an industry, your expert knowledge, your position relating to the business being covered in the story, and the value you offer as talent.

For example, if the media is looking to do a nice human interest piece on the latest design trends in bathrooms, they would be likely to target one or two of the following credible sources:

- The head of the Master Builders Association in their state to get an overview of how much bathroom builds or renovations cost, along with trends they're seeing emerging.

- A renowned plumber or builder who can offer an insight into what projects are popular at the moment.

- A bathroom and tiling retailer to find out what products are hot right now

- A well-known real estate salesperson to see what buyers want in bathrooms at the moment or whether they've recently sold any homes with a standout bathroom.

The journalist might speak to one of these sources, but it's more likely they'll go after two and what they'll be looking to achieve with their story is a picture of trends emerging.

Meanwhile, in a further example with more of a focus on hard news, just think back to Covid-19 news stories, especially those affecting small business like JobKeeper.

When initiatives like this were released, the media tended to use comments from the Prime Minister outlining what JobKeeper was and who it was aimed at, along with responses from small business representatives. **In this case, the small business talent they were after included:**

- Heads of small business associations like Chambers of Commerce representatives

- Actual business owners

- Staff members who would benefit

- Heads of workers organisations, such as the Hospitality Workers Union

Finding talent such as this allowed the media to create a story showing all sides of the issue.

So how do you become an expert or source the media actually seeks out?

Creating a Credible Profile

Your profile extends far beyond the information you send to the media and encompasses things like your website, LinkedIn profile and social media pages.

It relates to creating a profile and credibility that focusses on what you stand for. This credibility is the unique combination of skills and experiences that make you, YOU.

Ultimately honing this information into a simple concise message allows you to create consistent credibility statements across your media channels.

For example, if you are building credibility, you will need to ensure the About section of your website, social media channels and LinkedIn profile are consistent.

Meanwhile, this concise credibility description is further used for your media release boilerplate and an Available for Interview profile, both of which we will come to shortly.

Creating Credibility Statements

When considering your credibility, start with these questions:

- Who are you?
- What makes you unique?
- What is your vision for your business or personal brand?
- What are your professional goals?
- Who is your audience? Who can you help?
- How can you help them? What makes you different?
- What's your X Factor? What makes you reliable? Trustworthy?
- How do you prove that? What's the evidence?

In addition to these kinds of questions, start thinking about your accomplishments and gather any supporting materials that can reinforce them.

You can do this by:

- Writing out the accomplishments that make you proud

- Listing moments when others recognised you and your work publicly

- Thinking of times other people acknowledged your work privately

- Think holistically about what you are projecting and the impression that you want to leave with anyone who searches for you online.

Top tips for creating your credibility statement

List your attributes: This may seem a little bit too simple, but when you are trying to find some quality or skill that only you and a few other people have it really helps a lot.

The goal here is to find the one or two things that separate you from others and make you unique.

Choose an audience: Creating a statement that is too broad and is not directed at any particular group will most likely alienate journalists.

Since the purpose of a personal brand statement is to briefly list your primary skills, it is necessary to target the industry where those skills are most useful.

Be honest: It is tempting to exaggerate about your abilities, but this is not the place to do that. Don't say you're "the best" or a "leader in the field of..." unless you actually are.

Keep in mind that the credibility statement is only supposed to get people interested, and not say everything about your professional career.

Make it memorable: Even though you want it to stand out, remember that using excessively large or technical words may alienate your audience. Your credibility statement should be something that others can remember easily.

Try telling it to a friend or significant other one time and see if he or she can easily recall the entire sentence. If so, you're off to a good start.

Make your self–impression = other's impression: If you have trouble brainstorming personal skills, ask close friends or colleagues what they think your strengths are.

Even after you've decided on a statement, it is a good idea to check with a friend to make sure that your idea of yourself matches what others think of you.

The aim of the game here is to consolidate this information, ensure it is reflected across your website and social media, and to also use it specifically to target the media through tools like "Available for Interview" profiles and boilerplates.

Your Boilerplate Message

A boilerplate is a standardised paragraph inserted towards the end of a press release to add weight to the information you have provided.

It might be used to sum you up as an individual or provide a quick insight into your business.

No more than 100 words, a boilerplate is a short, succinct paragraph that helps explain who you are and what you do.

It is a standard addition to any release and should be carefully considered. The boilerplate is designed to highlight your value and your point of difference.

Journalists are estimated to receive anywhere between 50 and 500 press releases a week, and statistics indicate they take less than a minute to scan each

An easy-to-read, clear boilerplate is one of the key ingredients that can help you stand out from the crowd.

It effectively answers the questions: who is this from, why would I care, and how credible is this source?

So, a boilerplate at the end of a release might look like this.

"John Smith is a chartered accountant with 25 years' experience assisting small business. Working across sectors including retail, agriculture and hospitality, he is passionate about ensuring business operators understand their numbers in order to make more informed decisions."

Alternatively the boilerplate for a company might look like this...

"ABC Accounting works with some of the biggest names in small business, assisting business operators understand their numbers in order to make more informed decisions. A highly-regarded name in the industry, they have been serving the business community since 1995."

Creating Your Boilerplate

Although a boilerplate is a standardised paragraph, it might change depending on the goal you are trying to achieve at the time.

For example, a boilerplate might be designed to reflect your longevity, it might showcase your awards, or it might reflect your company culture and mission.

When creating a boilerplate, consider the following:

The Goal

What are you looking to highlight specifically – longevity? Awards? Culture?

An Explanation

A boilerplate always includes a succinct explanation of what the business or individual does.

This is a common structure for creating this explanation within a boilerplate:

"(Business name) creates (offering) to help (target audience) (solve a problem) with (differentiating characteristic)"

To help fill out these details, ask yourself:

- What industry is your business in?
- What does your business do?
- Who does your business work with?
- Where is your business located?
- When was your company founded?

- What size is your company? (employees, revenue and locations)
- Have you received any awards, commendations or recognition?

A Call to Action

Boilerplates always conclude with a call to action. In most cases this furnishes the journalist with the information they need to find out more about you. For example:

"ABC Accounting works with some of the biggest names in small business, assisting business operators understand their numbers in order to make more informed decisions. A highly-regarded name in the industry, they have been serving the business community since 1995.

You can learn more about ABC Accounting at abcaccounting. net.au."

An Available for Interview Profile

One highly effective way of gaining media attention is through an Available for Interview profile.

A bit like a press release but focused on outlining your expertise, rather than highlighting an event or issue, an Available for Interview submitted to journalists and allows them to understand what you may offer them as a source.

The aim of an Available for Interview is not to gain attention straight away (although this can happen), but instead to have the journalist or newsroom record your details as a potential expert they can use when a relevant story arises.

This Available for Interview extends on the credibility statement we talked about earlier. A lot like a bio, it involves outlining what makes you and your business an authority and unique.

In short, an "Available for Interview" profile allows you to showcase your expertise and business to the media.

Its purpose is to put you forward as talent they can call on when it comes to issues affecting your industry.

Available for Interview - *Insert Your Name* - What you are great at

Example: Available for interview - John Smith - Interior designer to the stars

Building Credibility with the critical first few paragraphs

The first few paragraphs of your Available for Interview Profile should introduce you, your expertise and give the journo a hook to interview you.

Example: With over 20 years' experience styling homes for the stars, John Smith brings an expert eye and all the latest inside tips on creating properties that exude style and quality.

His enviable and extensive client list includes Hollywood elite, world sporting greats and everyday Australians looking to create that perfect home environment to live in or for property sale.

About Business Name

A short paragraph then explains what your business does and why it is great at what it does.

Example: John Smith shares his expertise through his Sydney-based business Mr and Mrs Smith Star Styling, offering everyday Australians all the essential insight that allows them to create a welcoming home where "champagne taste" can be achieved on a "beer budget".

Why your name

Why should the Media pick you over other sources? This heading and paragraph help journalists who skim through a profile. It should be a short, sharp and snappy paragraph that says pick me.

Example: John Smith has styled the homes of some of the world's most renowned and fastidious stars.

He also boasts decades of industry expertise that enable him to identify the latest trends and provide tips on sourcing the right products to perfect a home.

Your name is available to discuss:

Your Name - is an expert in (mention your expertise again) and available for interview to discuss the following topics and much more:

In dot point list your top topics here to encourage and inspire the journalist to contact you.

Example: John Smith is renowned as one of the interior design industry's pre-eminent experts. He is available to discuss the following topics and more:

- What it's like to work with some of the world's most famous stars

- Selecting the right products to complete your home

- The latest interior design and furnishing trends

- Creating the right look on a limited budget

- Presenting homes for sale

For further information or to arrange an interview:

This is where you add your contact and connection details

- Name:
- Phone:
- Email:
- Website
- Social Links

Your Digital Footprint

In addition to creating a boilerplate and utilising Available for Interview profiles as a media tool, it's also critical the information you provide elsewhere matches up with what you say you offer in your press release.

That means paying attention to your website and your social media to ensure that credibility is also reflected there.

This helps create a complete picture of you as a credible source, because the media will search you elsewhere to verify who you are.

CHAPTER SIX

Working with Journalists

Working with journalists is the key to having your story conveyed.

To successfully work with the media, we need to understand that journalists live in an ever-changing world of deadlines and demands which can all alter in an instant.

What was destined to lead the front page in the morning may have changed numerous times by noon as events occur and announcements are made.

Work with your journalists to help get your story out there

If a journalist is swamped and has a tight deadline, offer to draft the piece for them.

But don't expect it will automatically run exactly as you have written it.

They will alter and edit items according to the style and tone of their publication and other restrictions including space.

Similarly, if you're handy with a camera, by all means provide a photograph. Ensure it's attention grabbing, of high resolution and would pique audience interest.

The key is to assist but not demand.

Respond to phone calls and emails quickly

Deadlines can arrive quickly and change swiftly in the media. The news moves fast and you need to too.

If you are calling a journalist, check if they are on deadline

If they are, offer to call back. And do call!

A quick rule of thumb is that daily newsrooms are best to contact in the morning, while weeklies and monthlies have more time in the days just after publication.

Give respect

Treat every journalist with respect. They have a job to do, editors to report to and deadlines to meet.

Sometimes news happens

Be aware that the media's schedule is determined by the "breaking" news of the day. Do not be offended if an interview gets cancelled or rescheduled because a more urgent story arises.

News is selective

Even though you have the most amazing idea for a story, it may not work for a publication or the timing may be wrong. It might work later - it just doesn't suit now.

Time is of the essence

If a journalist attends your event, be mindful of their time. It's rare they have more than an hour to physically attend a location. To assist, you should have briefing notes about the event handy and your talent available for immediate interview.

In your media alert or invitation to the event, advise the journalist of the best time to arrive so they will have these at their disposal. They need to get in, get out and get that story filed with any accompanying imagery.

Don't give up!

Working with Journalists Checklist

✓ Do you know which news outlets are likely to be most interested in your story?

✓ Do you know the name of the best journalist to contact in a newsroom regarding your story?

✓ Do you know their audience and the type of stories that appeal?

✓ Do you know their deadline?

✓ Can you provide usable images in the right resolution and size?

✓ Can you make yourself quickly available to answer any questions?

✓ If you are requesting a journalist attends an event, have you provided the best time for them to attend in order to speak with people, get images and get out quickly?

✓ Have you given them the information they need?

_____

_____

_____

_____

_____

_____

_____

CHAPTER SEVEN

Media Releases

Why use a media release?

With so many other marketing tactics, why would you choose to use a media release? Why should you devote the time and effort into crafting the perfect story, and then promoting it to various media outlets?

With the rise of the 24-hour newsroom, the need for a journalist to find stories and new sources is increasing, so media and press releases are a great way to get your story out there. When used within a well thought-out marketing strategy, a media release can provide a number of significant benefits to you and your business.

Exposure, awareness and branding

There are many opportunities to strengthen your brand with a media release. A media release is an excellent tool to help create awareness.

When used in conjunction with a strategic social media approach, your release can reach a larger, more engaged audience by attracting the attention of a journalist, blogger or media outlet.

Your media release can help you gain credibility through storytelling, case studies, and testimonials.

You can establish your authority in the industry with the information in your release.

Additionally, it's a great opportunity to communicate your message through extra information, links, and supporting content.

Increased website traffic

Why not incorporate some hyperlinks in the copy and create an interactive media release? These work especially well with online media.

When you send out your media release through various social media platforms and email, you have the opportunity to embed and integrate links.

When your release reaches your audience, many of them will click on the links and visit your website or blog.

It's important to make sure that the links in your media release support your goals for the release.

For example; if you want to drive traffic to an opt-in page and build your list then the link in your media release should go directly to your opt-in page.

Don't forget to double-check your links and test them before you send out the release!

Increased sales

By basing your marketing strategy around a media release, you can tap into buying triggers like credibility, authority, and likeability.

If you're using a media release to launch a new product or service, then you're likely to see a growth in sales.

You may experience this benefit even if you're not specifically trying to increase sales!

For example; a well-crafted announcement for an event or function may attract the attention of people who, in the process of learning more, decide to make a purchase while they're at it.

Media coverage

Let's not forget that if the media decides to pick up your story and cover your company, you will then have a tremendous opportunity to increase your branding, exposure, and sales.

For many, that's the ultimate goal for a media release and a solid marketing campaign.

The most important part of any media release is to ensure that it makes sense within the context of your business, your audience, your goals and your marketing.

When you're able to successfully integrate your releases into your existing marketing, you'll have a much larger return on investment and you'll reap the discussed benefits, and more.

Things to Consider when Writing a Release

Do your research: We all love facts and figures in an article but do make sure they are accurate and up to date.

Know your audience: Know the audience that you wish to reach and write directly for them.

Read the publications they read and use a similar approach when writing your release.

Think outside the box: Be creative with your release and think outside of the box. Different is good as it becomes attention grabbing.

Not every release needs to be or should be about a huge product or company announcement.

Sometimes it is the little unique things that make you attractive to the media. So, think outside the box and ask yourself what are you doing that is different?

Use online media: Online media has great social power to attract the right customers to your site.

One mention in the right blog, review or article can produce an effect worth tens of adverts. Online media is viral, shareable and moves fast so make sure you use it!

Know what is already being said about you: Google is an everyday journalism tool and often the first place a journalist will look.

Before you go to the media, do your research on you and know what is being said.

Use quotes: Sometimes a journalist won't be able to interview you, but they may still run the story if the press release has colour and contains key quotes from the people involved.

Brand your release: Images and logos build brand recognition for the journalist, so they become accustomed to you being an authoritative source.

Meanwhile, the media is becoming more and more visual so images and video count.

Be ready: For the calls once you send your release. You don't want to send a release and go away or into a meeting.

The media will move quickly if they are interested, so make sure you are ready with notes and know what to say.

_____

_____

_____

_____

_____

_____

_____

_____

The Makeup of a Media Release

Media releases comprise a number of standard elements, all of which are important to having your story told.

Different to academic or business writing, they incorporate attributed quotes and work in a reverse pyramid order where the most important information is at the beginning of the story and each paragraph beyond has information of lesser importance.

This occurs for a number of reasons: to grab the attention of the reader, so a newsroom can cut a story from the bottom up, so readers can skim articles and quickly attain the facts.

A Media Release Includes:

- An attention-grabbing headline

- A first paragraph revealing who, what, when, where, how or why

- Subsequent paragraphs working down through the order of important information

- Clear quotes attributed to an authority within your company

- Contact details for further information or interview

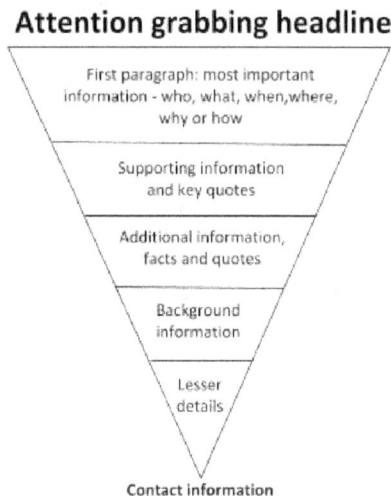

Attention grabbing headline

First paragraph: most important information - who, what, when, where, why or how

Supporting information and key quotes

Additional information, facts and quotes

Background information

Lesser details

Contact information

The fine print of a media release

It is the finer details of the media release, aka "fine print" that makes your release a success, so pay attention to these details.

Write a great headline

Your headline can make or break your release. It should be a short and snappy attention grabber. It should include points from your release and sum up its subject.

The headline is what encourages the media to read your release. Take your time and make it good.

It's important to note newsrooms receive hundreds of releases each day with the Editor or Chief of Staff making their decision on whether to pursue something in a matter of seconds. This makes your headline and first paragraph critical.

If you are emailing your release to a news outlet, ensure the headline is in the email subject line to give them a reason to click.

There are a host of handy tools to assist with creating headlines, and you can find them in detail in the resources section of this book.

Tell the story with your lead paragraph

The first paragraph is called "the lead". It is the most important part of the release and should contain the strongest key message.

This is where the who, what, when, where, and how or why of the story lives.

Journalists and Editors see lots of releases and may not read beyond the first paragraph. It is important that your lead includes all the necessary and relevant information.

Give them reason to read on.

Make your release editable

After the lead, each remaining paragraph should be less important than the one that precedes it. When your release is written this way, the story can, if necessary, be trimmed from the bottom up.

Each paragraph should be self-contained and regardless of how many paragraphs are deleted, the story should still make complete sense.

Keep your media release to one page (maximum 400-500 words).

The aim is to encourage a journalist to pursue your story, not to overwhelm or bore them with detail.

Allow the journalist to get to know and contact you

Finish with the media contact details and the company boilerplate.

The boilerplate is your media "elevator pitch". It summarises your business and product offerings to a reader who may have no prior knowledge of them.

This allows the journalist to get to know you and have the details they need to contact you.

Creating a boilerplate or bio

Creating your bio and boilerplate for your media releases is the key to your campaign.

When creating your bio include:

- What makes you unique

- What your key points of difference are

- Awards you have obtained/won

- The use of words and terms that describe you

As mentioned in Chapter Five, your bio and boilerplate are the credibility you offer to your release and article so take your time and make it good.

Using them consistently is part of your branding that allows the media to readily recognise who you are.

Proofread!

It is imperative you carefully proofread your media release and enlist the help of someone else to run their eye over it too.

You know what you're trying to say which increases the likelihood of only seeing what you expect, not what you have actually written.

A mistake in your release, even a small typo, can damage your credibility.

A good tip is to read twice; once for flow and the second time looking specifically at words and spelling.

Some of the best proofreaders even read backwards during this second read-through to easily see words independently of each other.

When proofreading be sure to double check:

The headline - Often typos are hidden here that the eye won't see.

Times and dates - If you are highlighting a time and date of an event, double check it! It's a common mistake to make errors with the time, day and even year.

Names - Ensure the name and title of anyone mentioned in your release is spelt correctly. This includes any specific journalists or editors you are addressing your release to.

Facts - Cross check any facts and figures.

Contact details - Cross check the email and phone numbers of any contacts listed, and also check hyperlinks.

Boilerplate and bio - Be sure to read over these as well.

Spell Check - Always run a spell check.

Your Release Checklist

✓ Does my headline stand out?

✓ Will the media open it? Is my release balanced? – does it inform as well as sell me?

✓ Is my release under one page?

✓ Does it have usable quotes?

✓ Are my images named to match my release and easy to find? Are captions provided?

✓ Are all my contact details in the release?

✓ Have I checked my release for jargon?

✓ Is my release readable and editable?

✓ Does the lead paragraph have the: how, who, what, where, when and why?

✓ Have I addressed the key benefits or values of my news?

✓ Have I considered how the readers will relate to this news?

✓ Are the facts current, correct and have I included and checked the accuracy of:

- spelling of names, organisations, products,

- job titles

- telephone numbers

- prices

- dates and times

- addresses

- contact details

✓ Has someone else read over my release to ensure there are no mistakes?

CHAPTER EIGHT

When to Write a Release

Throughout any given year there will be numerous occasions to write a media release. It's just a matter of finding them.

It's a great idea to plan out your year in advance, taking into account the triggers and events covered in this chapter.

Proactive Content and Sharing Good News

Proactive content involves sharing the achievements and events of your business. It says here we are and this is what we're doing.

Proactive content is found within the everyday operation of your business and includes:

When something new happens

When something is new it is always a great time to share it with the media.

The power of the next new thing is an alluring theme in marketing and PR.

The release of a new product or service

- A new website or significant upgrade to existing website
- Celebrating an important business anniversary

- The winning of a new client or engaging a new team member - (these announcements need the permission of both parties)

- A new staff member

- New premises

- A new logo

Ask Yourself: What is happening that is new in my business?

_____

_____

_____

_____

When you do something good

Doing something good not only feels good, it has great benefits in attracting the attention of the media.

Being involved with charity work or making a charitable contribution

- Releasing findings of new study or research

- Sponsoring an event or team, or individual

- Being singled out for an accomplishment or award within your field

- Establishing a scholarship or award for the local community

- You take on some pro bono work

Ask Yourself: Is something good happening in my business?

_____

_____

_____

_____

When you Grow

Business growth is a sign of growing credibility in your industry and the perfect time to share your news and expertise with the media.

It includes:

- Starting a new division or sister company/business

- Partnering with another business or organisation

- When you open a new location

- Adding a new brand or product

- Taking on a partner or listing on the stock market

Ask Yourself: What growth is happening/about to happen in my business?

_____

_____

_____

_____

When you have Something to Share

There are many sharable moments in any business – from exciting milestones to new initiatives, and these offer a prime opportunity to illustrate what you do.

- Offering free information: eBook, newsletter or webinars

- Announcing a media appearance

- Changing the way your products are made

- Developing a new technology or different procedure for your industry

- Celebrating an important milestone

- You are exhibiting at or holding a trade show

- Speaking at a conference or event

- Receiving endorsements from a celebrity, industry or public figure (ensure you gain the appropriate permissions)

Ask Yourself: What news do we have to share?

_____

_____

_____

_____

_____

_____

_____

_____

_____

_____

_____

_____

_____

Reactive Reasons and Using the News

There's a reason it's called a news cycle. News has the innate ability to breed news and this is where reactive PR comes into play.

Reactive media engagement usually relates to something that someone else says or does which prompts you to comment.

Tying your news into a current news story increases the chances of it being seen, simply because it is newsworthy.

The key is to act quickly, think like a newsroom and get your story out fast.

The sooner you respond, the more likely your story will be incorporated into coverage of an issue.

And when we say act quickly, that means within hours, not days.

Meanwhile, there are a host of ways to use reactive media releases to great effect.

_____

_____

_____

_____

_____

_____

_____

_____

When you Support Something

A prime time to get in on the media action is when an industry body or government sector releases an initiative or statement your business ethos supports.

Your releases then revolve around the following:

- Why this move is a good idea

- Who it affects and how it impacts them positively

- What your business does that supports this push and makes you an authority

Ask Yourself: Does this initiative significantly benefit my audience, why and how?

_____

_____

_____

_____

_____

_____

_____

When you Disagree with Something

Conversely, a contentious issue or one that will cause harm to your sector is also an ideal time to make your case.

Your releases then focus around:

- Why this move is a bad idea

- Who it affects and how it impacts them adversely

- What your business does that is contrary to this push and why you are an authority

Ask Yourself: Does this initiative significantly negatively impact my audience, why and how?

_____

_____

_____

_____

_____

_____

_____

When you can contribute to a debate (or ride the news wave)

Weighing in on a media debate involves using your position or authority within a sector to add meaningful dialogue. It involves:

- Providing a possible alternative to an issue
- Offering tips and advice for those affected
- Telling the story of how your industry or sector is affected

A couple of Readily Recalled News Examples

Much of the Australian news in 2014 was devoted to the carbon tax. It was a heady debate that had the potential to impact many.

Reactive releases at the time could have added to the debate by discussing:

- How politicians could have negotiated
- Alternative ways for the tax debate to play out
- Sharing stories of those affected by the carbon tax removal.
- Top tips for families on what to look for post carbon tax.
- What no carbon tax meant for business
- What the public needed to know that politicians may have been hiding

At around the same the mystery disappearance of Malaysian Airlines flight MH17 was also playing out in the media.

Topics to consider in that instance would have included:

- Assisting the families with grief support
- Advice on helping children cope with the images they were seeing on the news.
- Resources that loved ones can access, etc.

Ask Yourself: What can I add to this topic as an authority that hasn't already been covered?

_____

_____

_____

_____

_____

_____

_____

_____

_____

_____

_____

_____

When someone says something about you

Arguably, the prime reason for a reactive media release is when someone else says something about you in the media, either good or bad.

In the instance of negative publicity releases may involve:

- Refuting claims

- Explaining circumstances

- Accepting criticism, noting where improvements will be made, that an investigation is pending and reiterating the core values of your brand.

- Highlighting other achievements

Ask Yourself: How can I limit damage, explain the situation and have my business seen in a better light?

_____

_____

_____

_____

_____

_____

In the welcome instances where it's public praise, releases involve:

- Welcoming the feedback
- Highlighting your good record
- Focusing on positive business partnerships
- Reiterating the core values of your brand

Ask Yourself: How can I maximise exposure, build business credibility and have my business seen in an even better light?

_____

_____

_____

_____

_____

_____

_____

_____

_____

Ongoing Reasons and Evergreen Content

Evergreen content is always fresh – it can be used at any time throughout the year, or is fresh at a certain time, year after year after year.

In a nutshell, it is content that stays relevant to your readers and/or the media.

So where do you find evergreen content in your business?

Evergreen angles are easier to find than you think. They are hidden within your knowledge, and often they are the things you take for granted as being "known" about your industry.

Evergreen content is:

- Your top five tips on a topic

- Tips for beginners

- Explaining industry terms

- Checklists

- Infographics

- How to use your products or services

- Ideas and resources

- Best tools for your audience (free and paid are always good)

- Things you should know or questions to ask.... (before using a service for example)

- Answer the questions you are being asked by clients. They are your audience, and what they want to know, others will too.

- Share your secrets... by giving a secret away, it creates credibility and creates the need to want to know more

The important thing about being evergreen with your content is to mix it in with current and topical pieces as well. Do not flood the press or your blog all at once.

Media Release Ideas and Tips

Share helpful tips

Tips enable you to educate your market, providing timely and welcome advice relating to their needs, your business, or your services and products.

For example, they might be:

- The top ten, or five tips to succeed in your industry
- Tips for clients and customers on how to use your products or services
- Advice for people starting out in your field
- Tips sheets or feature stories around events and holidays that relate to your business e.g. Christmas, Valentine's Day, Tax Time etc.

Share something unusual

Is there some interesting or unusual thing, event, or circumstance about your business or industry that you can share, e.g.:

- The world's biggest...
- World First...
- Did you hear about...

Market trends and thought leadership

Position yourself as the expert by commenting on market trends and issues that affect your industry:

- Comment on or tie into current events and interesting trends
- Industry predictions - make them
- Comment on findings of a recent report, survey or poll
- Debunk common myths about products or services

Putting yourself out there allows the media to get to know you:

- Offer your product or service for review. It is great exposure for your brand

- Run market research on your business and why people use you and publish the findings

- Use your quiet time of year. Start writing an article bank that you can submit when the need arises

- Add to a story that is already in the media

Mapping out your Media Year

The following activity will help you plan for your media year using evergreen and proactive techniques, along with flagging potential events to react to.

Some people use a spreadsheet for this, others a calendar, but the key is to be ahead of the game in the knowledge that releases often need to go out in advance.

1. Go through a calendar and flag dates for evergreen content. Depending on your industry these could include:

   - New Year's resolutions

   - Australia Day

   - Back to school

   - Valentine's Day

   - Easter

   - School holidays

   - Public holidays

   - Awareness days for health like World's Greatest Shave or Pink Ribbon Day

   - End of Financial Year

   - Halloween

- Christmas
- New Year's festivities

2. Go through your business activities for the year and flag any events on your calendar for proactive content.

   This will evolve throughout the year, but could include:

   - A product launch
   - A sale
   - A change in premises
   - An event
   - Attendance at a third party event
   - An awards ceremony

3. While reactive PR tends to revolve around current news, there will be times throughout the year when you are more likely to comment.

Note these on your calendar as well, such as:

   - Dates of industry body annual meetings
   - Political elections
   - Federal or state budgets
   - Dates that report findings are due

4. Using this information, create a spreadsheet or list of ideas for articles to write across the year.

5. In your spare time or during the traditionally quiet business months of January and February, create an article bank of pre-written content.

Things in Your Media Year:

_____

_____

_____

_____

_____

_____

_____

_____

_____

_____

_____

_____

_____

_____

_____

_____

_____

_____

_____

_____

_____

_____

_____

_____

_____

CHAPTER NINE

Finding Ideas and Creating a Strategy

Your next media release is often hiding inside your day. What is topical and current is there - you just need to find it.

Where to Look:

- Today's paper – your next story idea may be in there

- Your blog – the story you tell your clients if often news

- Your newsletter

- Your competitors - what are they saying and doing?

- What are your staff talking about? Is there an industry trend or topic making office gossip?

- The questions your clients are asking – can you answer them in a release that educates the public?

Work Out Loud

This concept was coined by John Stepper and encourages people and businesses to talk about what they are currently working on through social media, post-it notes or just by chatting about it.

This promotes more efficiency and happiness at work as people get connected with others who can share, promote and help them through their work, forming new collaborations and networks.

The same applies when looking for release ideas within your business. "Work Out Loud" and share what you are doing with the media so they get to "know" you!

Are you releasing a new product or range?

Share with the media what it is, what makes it special and why you are launching it.

Alternatively, you could test the waters by asking for feedback on your ideas through social media.

Have you been nominated for or won an award?

Be your own champion and shout about it! After all, it is award season so now is a great time to boost your credibility by sharing your award news.

Why not send links to other competitions you are in the running for or publicise your other products to give your business more exposure?

Are you planning an event?

What if you have been planning an event for months and the big day is just around the corner?

Perhaps it's just a coffee morning or a simple workshop, no matter what it is, invite the media along to see you in action.

Likewise, local newsrooms love local stories, so if you are doing something good locally shout about it!

Are you a travel or tourism business?

Get creative and put together a special media tour package with everything from photos to videos to showcase what you do.

Share your story

You might not think it's very interesting, but perhaps the road of your business history is paved with all sorts of weird and wonderful stories.

Get them out there and share them, you never know – your story could inspire someone else.

Cheer on your employees.

Share any successes or triumphs, no matter how big or small, in a release. They'll be happier and in turn, so will you.

Is this your client's busy season?

Share some tips on how your services can make their life easier. They will thank you for putting them first.

Do people know what you do?

Education is a great way to attract media attention, why not explain what it is you do and why it works.

Keep it simple and let people know whenever you update a service or procedure and keep abreast of industry happenings by keeping active socially – people trust businesses who are transparent and on the ball.

Don't Forget the Why Behind your Brand

Run a quick internet search for any consumer service and the results will astound you, with pages and pages of businesses all competing in the same area for the same market.

Their products may be the same, their premises may look alike, their customer service top notch.

So what is the point of difference that will see customers select one business over another?

More often than not it is the "why" behind the brand, and the "why" is a story every business should take the time to tell.

Each business has a unique reason for why they do what they do and how they came to do it.

Telling this story to the media and consumers provides a critical insight into who you are and what you offer.

The internet has made sharing the why behind your business easier with about pages, staff profiles, blogs and more to give a history of a company and allow consumers to form connections.

It is the "why" that makes a service personal, relatable and unique.

But it's also a vital component in public relations strategy as a whole, giving the public a reference point when they consider your services and industry.

"Oh that's Joe's plumbing, he's a third generation plumber whose family has worked in town since the days when outhouses were still around."

"Wholesome Whole Foods – I know them – the woman who started that built her business from a market stall when her children were small and it's now it a national distributor of Australian-made products."

This back story (the why behind the brand) is often more intriguing than any product or service on offer, establishing a personal connection in an impersonal world.

And it is that "why" that allows clients, the public and the media to connect with you.

CHAPTER TEN

Building your Media List

Your media list is a critical document that allows you to easily connect with the right people, quickly.

It should be kept current and added to regularly.

Use social media to network with journalists

Start by following key journalists in your industry on social media channels including Twitter, Facebook, Pinterest and Google+.

Follow the outlets too, so you can see the story trends and tailor an article or two just for them.

Research journalists

Determine which demographic and publications have the audience who would be interested in your release. Look at their writing style and what appeals to their readers. Note these things down on your list.

Organise and categorise your list

Make sure your list is organised with all the details you need e.g.: phone, email, the preferred method of pitching, the best time to call etc.

Look after your list

Your list is a valuable tool, look after it. Update it. Add to it and nurture the relationships you have within it.

And remember, these are relationships you have on this list, so respect their details.

Take advantage of newspaper and magazine editorial calendars

Editorial calendars help you to know which topics will be featured in which issues.

Use these to research and add the right topics to your plan, your campaigns and contact lists.

Remembering to keep planning ahead of time.

Become a reliable resource

Always provide accurate information on time.

Make the effort to get to know your local media as they are often hungry for local news stories, which is you!

Ask if you can help with stories around an upcoming event or topic. Pitch only what you know is needed and be available.

Distributing a release

Get your news out to the media quickly by distributing your release.

Release distribution allows you to reach a number of journalists at once, increasing the chances of it being picked up.

Release distribution is a fast and efficient way to share your story.

There are many tools out there to help you distribute your releases. It is about finding the ones that are right for you.

Email distribution

Email distribution is a great way to connect with the journalists you already know.

The key to this is making sure your list is up-to-date and that you have permission to send releases through.

Newsrooms and alert services

Newsrooms and Alert services do the networking with the media for you. They create the media lists, send and promote your release for you.

What do you choose?

A mix – newsrooms and alert services bring new journalists to you while your lists connect you with media you have already worked with.

_____

_____

_____

_____

_____

_____

_____

_____

_____

_____

_____

_____

_____

_____

_____

Pitching a Story

A well-written tailored pitch tells a journalist "I know who you are, I know what you cover and I can add value to your audience". Pitching a release takes time but it is a tailored and more strategic approach that entices journalists.

Know how to pitch

Know how your journalist likes to work before pitching your release.

If you don't know and you call journalists who absolutely hate phone calls, or pitch them on a site like Facebook, which they use only for staying in touch with family and friends, you risk alienating them.

If you don't know - don't pitch.

Keep it brief

If calling, make your pitch short and sweet – let the journalist say yes or no to hearing more. If pitching via email, just a few sentences about the story idea with an attached release will do.

Make them want to contact you

Your pitch needs to give enough information to be enticing, but not so much that it's too hard to read.

The best pitch promises a great story and entices the recipient to contact you to learn more.

Reverse Pitching

Reverse Pitching is when a journalist asks you to pitch your ideas to them either via email or media sites like HARO, Sourcebottle etc.

A journalist will normally 'call out' for pitches when they are on a deadline, so being quick and making things easy is the key.

Be quotable

Use quotes to make the job as easy as possible for the journalist.

The journalist may be under deadline pressure and need a quick fill piece. Give them bite sizes snippets that make it easy to quote you.

You can get quoted without ever speaking to a journalist so make the most of this opportunity.

Reply quickly

Reverse pitches need you to be quick. Journalists have deadlines and the key is to respond quickly to be in the lead.

Read the request

When reverse pitching, it is really important to read the request and address it in your response.

Questions to ask before Reverse Pitching

Do I really fit what this journalist is looking for in a source?

If the answer is no, then do not offer yourself. It can be tempting to pitch anyway especially when it's a major outlet or an outlet that you would love to be in.

But to work, the fit needs to be there and if it isn't, all you do is risk alienating a journalist.

Would I pitch to this publication had I not seen the request?

The topic might be so right for you but the outlet may not be.

Take a step back and review if the fit works for you. If not, then don't submit.

What's the "Takeaway" of your story?

Why would the journalist choose you for this story? Give them a takeaway to grab hold of, to make them want to contact you.

CHAPTER ELEVEN

Interviews

The Interview Be's

The key to an interview is the "Be": being ready, being prepared and being professional.

These factors make all the difference.

Be ready

Once you send a release be ready for the interview. Expect journalists to call.

Be professional

Inviting the media to contact you means you need to be professional. Answer the phone, dress and act professionally.

Be prepared

Prepare in advance two or three key ideas and points you want to cover. Be the journalist as you prepare and think of questions you would ask.

Be honest

Always tell the truth. If you don't and try to bluff, you will be found out.

Journalists are excellent at uncovering bluffers.

If you don't know an answer, say so, and offer to find out and provide them the information quickly after the interview.

Be brief

Time is important in an interview. Keep your statement brief and complete so if necessary the interview can be edited down.

Be you

Keep your voice at an even pace. Act naturally. They are interviewing you because they wanted YOU!

Be energetic

Use gestures, facial expressions and body language to add vitality and emphasis to what you are saying.

Be focused

Direct your full attention on the interviewer. Look at the person asking the questions and engage them.

Preparing for an interview

Note the deadline

Understand that journalists are usually working to a deadline. Return calls as soon as you can. Ask about deadlines and meet or beat them.

Know who you are talking to

Ask for the journalist's name and what publication/outlet they are reporting for. If the person or media outlet is unfamiliar to you, ask for a bit more detail on the audience reach and demographic.

Know what you want to say

Be prepared for an interview. Know what you want to say in your interview.

Think of two or three main points you would like to make about your subject.

Gather facts, figures and anecdotes to support your points. Anticipate questions the journalist might ask and have your responses ready.

Keep it simple

Try to avoid unnecessarily wordy phrases in an interview with the media and keep what you're saying clear and simple.

Be prepared

Whenever possible, have any printed materials on hand to support your story in order to help the journalist minimise errors.

If time allows, offer to send a copy to the journalist.

During your interview

Ask if you are being recorded

If you are being interviewed by phone, ask if you are being recorded. Ask if the interview is live.

Also find out if the interview will be edited. And only agree to a live interview if you are comfortable thinking on your feet and responding off the cuff.

Avoid jargon

Avoid academic or technical jargon; if you must use them, explain the terms you use.

Make your comments count

We live in the age of the sound bite. Television and radio stories may use only a 10-30 second cut.

The shorter your comments, the less likely they are to be edited. Even print journalists are looking for short, snappy quotes.

Stay on message

Keep to your main points and do not allow yourself to get drawn too far off on tangents.

Speak in complete thoughts. The journalist's question may be edited out, and your response should stand on its own.

Explain and ask for explanation

Don't overestimate a journalist's knowledge of your subject.

When a journalist bases a question on information you believe is incorrect, don't hesitate to politely set the record straight and offer background information.

If you do not understand a question, ask for clarification. If you do not have the answer, say so. Giving a false answer only reflects badly on you.

Stay still

Any movement in an audio interview can change the sound quality. Stay still in front of radio or TV microphones and avoid sitting in a chair that rocks or spins.

Wandering around or rocking in your chair can cause the recorded volume to rise and fall. And tapping pens and feet make noise too.

Don't go off the record

It sounds exciting but telling a journalist you'd like to say something "off the record" is never a good idea.

Off the record is an individual moral code that some journalists believe in and others do not.

In the end, the media is all about the story and information that you provide off the record can end up being published anyway. If you think it should be off the record - don't say it!

Radio interviews

Radio interviews are all about the audio so the quality needs to be good and your message clear.

Find the best place

If you are being interviewed via the phone, make sure you are in a place where you can be heard, the signal is strong, and your battery is charged.

Reduce the chance of noise

Avoid shuffling paper, clicking pens or tapping your feet. Take off any earrings etc. that can make a noise against the phone.

Turn your mobile phone off. Switching it to silent mode still won't stop the electronic interference.

There is nothing worse than a phone ringing during an interview.

Don't forget to also turn off any radio in the background.

If it's a live radio interview and their station is playing in the background, it produces an echo.

Give them audio they can use

Make editing easy by pausing when you complete a point. This allows for producers to get promotional sound grabs too.

Avoid statements such as "Like I said earlier" etc. as it makes the audio harder to edit and your key statement could be missed.

Talk slowly and breathe. You want to make your points clearly, so make sure you take a breath and take the time to say what you want to say.

Know what you want to say

Have notes that you can refer to, allowing you to focus and refocus on the interview.

TV interviews

The TV Interview is all about engaging the interviewer and audience. It's also about appearance.

Know where to look

Look at the journalist and not the camera.

The only exception is in a remote interview, when the interviewer may not be on location.

If you're uncertain where to look, ask and the producer, journalist or camera operator will tell you.

Know what to wear

The visual nature of TV means that solid, bright colours work best on screen.

Don't wear light-sensitive glasses. Studio lighting will make your glasses darker and viewers won't be able to see your eyes. Avoid big shiny jewels that will reflect the light.

Keep makeup natural and "you". Your everyday makeup should do. Look in the mirror, if possible, just before going on camera.

The journalist may not notice that your collar is folded over, or your hair is out of place.

Bear in mind that fabrics with close stripes can cause a strobing effect.

Know what to say

Rehearse and plan what you are going to say. Be prepared for the questions you don't want.

Read over your notes before going on air. But don't during an interview; only refer to them if you get "stuck".

Know what to do

Be aware of and avoid nervous habits such as pen tapping or other behaviour that can interfere with sound quality.

Deliver your message with confidence. After all, you know more about the topic than the interviewer.

Stay seated and silent when the interview is over. You might still be on camera and trip over a wire or do something else awkward.

Never say anything that you don't expect to go to air, even after the interview appears to be over. Even professional anchors have been caught out making asides they didn't realise were live.

Outdoor interviews can present challenges of their own including wind and stray flies.

The key is to keep calm and carry on but don't pretend it's not happening. Do hold your hair out of your face or swat away the fly if necessary.

Bringing the interview back to you

Journalists are great at pushing a story where they want it to go. If the story is not heading the way you want, have a few of these bridging statements ready to bring the interview back to you:

- "I think it would be more accurate (or correct) to say...
- "We find the more important issue is..."
- "Let me emphasise again..."
- "And that reminds me..."
- "What matters most in this situation is..."

- "While...is important, it's also important to remember that..."

- "Before we leave this subject, I need to add..."

Tricky Interviews

Not all interviews are easy and not all reasons for agreeing to an interview are pleasant, which makes handling tricky interviews a good skill to have up your sleeve.

Hard interviews are most likely to occur if you're a contentious public figure like a politician or your business is in damage control.

While most politicians are well versed at hard interviews, for business operators it takes a little more getting used to, so here are some tips.

Seek advice

If you are facing a major business crisis that is being played out publicly, seek advice.

That may include legal advice about what you can and cannot say, the advice of your partners and board members or the advice of a professional media strategist.

Bear in mind if the matter is subject to, or likely to be subject to any legal proceedings or investigation there will be limitations to what you can say.

Know your message

Contentious issues call for a clear and concise response and you need to map out precisely what that will be.

Your aim is to reflect your business in the best possible light while also acknowledging the issue at hand.

A clear example that many will recall was the fatal accident a Dreamworld in 2016.

The immediate message in that instance should have been:

- Confirmation of a tragic event at Dreamworld

- Conveying sympathy to the families and those affected

- Offering all available assistance and support to investigators

- Indicating little more could be said about the specifics of the incident as an investigation was under way

- Noting Dreamworld's commitment to patron safety

- Indicating staff and management were also deeply affected

- Announcing, in addition to the investigation, there would be an internal safety review

The best person for the job

Fronting the media during damage control is not an easy task, so ensure you select the right person for the job.

This person needs to be calm under pressure, convey the company's message clearly, and deflect any questions that cannot or should not be answered.

This person may not be you, it could be your lawyer or a carefully selected business spokesperson.

It does need to be someone in a position of authority.

Keep calm, remain polite

At all times remain calm and polite, even if you have answered the same question multiple times, or are being asked something you cannot reasonably or legally answer.

We'll provide tips on exactly how to do this in the next section, but remember that one moment of losing your composure could be the exact item that's used in the news, so do not provide the media with this opportunity.

If in doubt, put out a statement

It's not the ideal response but if you have doubts about your ability to handle an issue, seek advice and release a statement.

This is a much better option than the alternative of doing nothing at all.

Ensure your company actions back your words

It almost goes without saying but your business should be careful of what it does during a period of damage control.

This is not a time to be seen hosting lavish parties or releasing company bonuses.

Again Dreamworld is a good example. After failing to hit the right message of sympathy and contrition with the public, they went on to host an AGM which included the announcement of annual bonuses. Not a good look.

Your business actions should support the message you have conveyed to the media.

Staying on message

Whether it's during damage control, as part of a debate or just handling a tenacious journalist, there are a host of ways to effectively deflect, get back on topic and handle tetchy interviews with ease.

It all comes down to the bridging statement, and here's how to pull it off with panache.

The bridging statement

Bridging statements are all about taking or regaining control of an interview.

Their role is to refocus the reporter (and their audience) on your message, keeping it clear, concise, and memorable.

While regularly used in fiery interviews such as when politicians are being taken to task, the role of bridging statement extends far beyond damage control and pork barrelling.

Done well, they will keep an interview "on message" in a calm manner that sees your desired information come across even after an editing process.

The main aim

The aim of the bridging statement is to keep focus on your most important message, and that means having it at the forefront of your mind before and throughout the interview.

As the talent being interviewed, you should be acutely aware of exactly the information you wish to impart, have the facts and figures that back it up at hand, and have a number of ways to say it up your sleeve.

You should also know your limitations and not be tempted to overstep the mark.

Use the bridging statement to indicate that's not an area where you can comment, before bringing the interviewer back to your topic of discussion.

The key to delivery

While the bridging statement may be used to handle tricky interviews or contentious issues, the key is to deliver it consistently in a calm, approachable and unflappable manner.

The following are great examples of bridging statements that can be applied to almost any interview situation.

Bridging statement examples

When asked a question you cannot answer

- I'm sorry, I don't have the precise details. I will come back to you on that.

- I'm sorry, I am unaware of that. However, what I can say is...

When asked a question you should not answer

- I won't speculate. What matters in this situation is..."

- I'm not here/able to comment on that. What I would like to say is...

- What you're talking about isn't my area of expertise, what I can say is...

- You wouldn't expect me to discuss such sensitive issues with the media before talking to staff ...

- I cannot speak for xxx, you should address issues to them specifically. What I can say is ...

When you think something is being misconstrued

- I think it would be more accurate (or correct) to say...

- While... is important, it's also important to remember that...

- I think it would be more correct to say...

- Let me point out again that...

- Let me emphasise again...

- In this context, it is essential that I note...

- Before we continue, let me take a step back and repeat that...

- Before we continue, let me emphasise that...

- Here's the real issue...

- While...is important, it is also important to remember...

- It's true that...but it is also true that...

When the interview is going off-topic

- Before we leave this subject, I need to add..."

- Another thing to remember is...

- Before we leave the subject, let me add that...

- What matters most in this situation is...

- Here's the real problem...

- And that reminds me..."

- However, what is more important to look at is...

- However, the real issue here is...

- Let me just add to this that...

- When the journalist is missing a key point

- We find the more important issue is...

- What I've said comes down to this...

- Let me emphasise again...

- It all boils down to this..."

- And what's most important to know is..."

- If we take a broader perspective...

- And what this all means is...

- And what's most important to remember is...

- With this in mind, if we look at the bigger picture...

- With this in mind, if we take a look back...

- The key here is...

- I'd also like to add that...

- If we look at the big picture...

- Let me put all this in perspective by saying...

- What all this information tells me is...

- This is an important point because...

- What this all boils down to is...

- The heart of the matter is...

- What matters most in this situation is... And if we take a closer look, we would see...

- Just to put this into some context ...

- What's absolutely critical to remember is...

- To put this in perspective ...

- The point is...

- And that reminds me...

- And the one thing that is important to remember is...

- What I'm most concerned about is...

- What we have to look at is...

When things get argumentative

- People have said that but...

- I can't agree with you

- I see that, but ... (key message)

- That's very interesting, but first let me make the point...

- That's very interesting, but what I believe is...

- Have you visited the site/seen the building/tested the equipment you are criticising – I'd be delighted to show you...

When interrupted

- And as I said before...

- What I've said comes down to this:..

- May I finish the point I was making...

- You've asked an important question and I would like the opportunity to answer

Interview Checklist

✓ Do you know who is interviewing you and what the audience of the media outlet is?

✓ How will this interview be used? Are you the only source, or one of many?

✓ Will this interview be live or taped?

✓ For a television interview, are you ready to make your appearance?

    o   What will you wear?

    o   What about use of makeup?

✓ If time allows, have you rehearsed all possible questions and answers with someone else?

✓ Can you explain your points in a concise manner?

✓ Do you have the notes for your own reference?

✓ Can you present your information in an honest, efficient way without industry jargon?

After the Interview

Give them the information they need to know about you

Tell the journalist how you wish to be identified, e.g. your name, title and any qualifications you may have.

Do spell your first and last name for them regardless of how simple it may be.

Even "Smith" can be spelt two ways.

Offer to fact check

Make yourself available to check the article's key facts. It invites the journalist to come back to you to make sure the facts of the story are clear.

This doesn't mean you will get to see an advance copy of an article.

There are few, if any, circumstances where a journalist will provide you with a story prior to publication.

However, by making yourself available to answer any questions or confirm any details, you are assisting in ensuring the accuracy of their story.

Get an idea of when the story will appear

Ask when your story is likely to appear, so you don't end up hounding the journalist with 100 emails.

Replay the interview

Replay the interview in your head and if you think that you misspoke or gave incorrect information, call the journalist as soon as possible and let them know.

If an error does appear, let the journalist know right away in a polite and respectful manner.

Sometimes a correction can be printed or aired. Bear in mind a journalist's job depends on accuracy, but mistakes do happen in the fast-paced environment of news.

Share your media coverage

When you get media coverage, share the love! By sharing media coverage you will help raise the profile of your business and the journalist. Journalists are grateful when their work is recognised and shared.

Express appreciation

If you genuinely think a journalist did an excellent job telling your complex story or fairly relating the facts, tell them via a quick email or call. Appreciation goes a long way.

Archive and keep a copy

Keep a copy of your magazine and newspaper coverage. Be sure to keep the masthead.

Take a screenshot of online interviews and coverage. For radio and TV stories, obtain a tape of the interview. Most outlets are happy to provide one.

_____

_____

_____

_____

_____

_____

_____

_____

CHAPTER TWELVE

Article & Blog Writing

Article writing is a must for your PR toolkit. Whether it's a blog, guest post on a third-party website, newsletter or other publication, it builds credibility and creates your profile as an expert, while giving the media and publications a chance to get to know you.

Article writing differs from media releases as all the information comes from you minus the involvement of an interview or journalist.

Basically, you provide it in the style that it will generally run with all the elements incorporated.

The online media has a wealth of opportunities when it comes to placing quality articles, and this is a very real way to build the profile of your brand.

Like a news release, articles features facts, research and even occasional quotes.

Here's what You Need to Know:

Who are you writing for?

When writing your articles, just like releases, you need to know who you are writing for:

The reader (who is the reader you want to attract?)

The publication (what is the style of the publication?). By doing some research and getting to know the publication and its readers before submitting, your articles increase their chances of being run.

Know your audience and write for them

Readers want to learn something new that is important and relevant to them.

Your article needs to offer that 'something' new for the reader such as information, tips, advice, resources, or benefits. Give readers reasons to read and they will.

Article Writing Tips

Use journalistic style

A well-written article will reflect a news-style of writing. The five W's and H (who, what, where, when, why, and how) should all be contained in an interesting opening statement.

The remaining information should be answered in the following paragraphs.

Include research quotes, facts, & statistics

Research and gather any necessary facts, conduct interviews, find resources, etc.

Use direct quotes from interviews and supplement articles with interesting facts and statistics.

Keep it simple

You want to engage your reader, not confuse them. Avoid using jargon or expressing personal opinions, except in direct quotes.

Make it easy to read

Keep your article to the point and easy to read. Use bullets, lists, short sentences, and lots of paragraphs.

Be visual

Choose pictures/images that will enhance your article. In the world of social sharing, visual and images win out.

Make the title count

Your title is what will get the reader to read on. Make it count. Ensure your title stands out and says "read me!"

Follow the style guide

There is no point in writing a great article only to have it rejected because you did not follow the style guide.

By following the guide, you are also more likely to engage and connect with the outlet's readers.

_____

_____

_____

_____

_____

Blog Writing Tips

Blog writing is an essential element of any PR strategy, and it offers a host of benefits to businesses that choose to embrace it.

Like any PR, it should be done regularly with a new blog post weekly, fortnightly or monthly.

As it's placed on your own website, a company blog offers you complete control of what you want to say, when, and how you wish to say it.

Other benefits include:

- Building client engagement with your brand
- Creating a position of authority in your industry
- A more personalised communication tool
- Sharing and viral potential
- Search engine optimisation to shift your website up the Google ranks

Like a news release, blogs can be based on proactive, reactive or evergreen content, but the key is to keep them regular.

Meanwhile the structure and tone can be less formal than a news release or article.

As blog writing is all about getting people to keep coming back to you and click on the new content, tips, advice and "listicles" are great tools to use, such as...

- "Three things every business owner should know"
- "Five reasons this Federal Budget will benefit families"
- "10 tips for a professional interior paint job"
- "Five ways to eat well this summer"
- "Top tech trends"

The Structure of a Blog Post:

The blog offers a more personal connection with your audience, which means its tone can pose an argument, and it can be written in the first person from your position of authority.

The first paragraph usually starts with a universal statement or fact that clearly sets out your theory and highlights where you're heading, and then the body is broken down into easily read components under subheadings.

After outlining your sage advice or tips on the matter, a blog usually concludes with a final roundup, a call to action and link to your product or services.

The average length of a blog is about 400-500 words.

For example, this would be a typical blog for a tutoring company:

"Five signs your child may need a tutor"

Intro:

No parent wants to see their child struggling at school. (Fact and problem your business can solve) But the good news is the sooner you address any academic challenges, the faster you can set your child back on track and re-instil the confidence they need to thrive in the classroom. (Desired result and solution)

Here are the five top signs your child may need a tutor...(Lead in to the authoritative advice you're about to offer)

(Then launch into the following subheads explaining each)

Subheads:

- Their grades are slipping
- Homework is a hassle
- Your child doesn't want to go to school
- They seem withdrawn
- They are easily frustrated

Conclusion:

It's hard to watch your child suffer but the sooner you recognise the signs of struggle, the better placed you are to change their academic future (roundup).

At Acme Tutoring we have 50 years' experience working with children to achieve their academic goals using one on one expert tutoring techniques (about you).

You can contact us here (link to you) for further advice or peruse our unique tutoring packages (link to your product).

The Value of Blogs

Used well, blogs can position your business as an authority in an industry where people come to seek advice.

Try and keep the topics varied across your field or expertise. It's a great idea to establish a bank of topics or even complete articles that you can refer to and work with throughout the year.

_____

_____

_____

_____

_____

_____

_____

_____

_____

_____

_____

CHAPTER THIRTEEN

The Basic Ingredients of Good PR

Like it or loathe it, maintaining a media profile and promoting your product or services is a major component of modern business.

That means taking the time each week to work your media and PR strategy. Yes, it's easier said than done but these few points will help you keep on track.

Keep Your Eyes Wide Open

It's in the interests of every business to keep an eye on news that may relate to them, whether that's the competition launching a product, government initiatives that may impact your industry or technological innovations that may affect the way you do business.

Most importantly, relevant news may provide a timely opportunity for your business to comment on an issue and raise your profile. Each day, business should have its ear to the ground for new developments.

Blog Weekly - Guest Blogging or your Own Site

Blogs are only just beginning to use their power in Australia, but the potential is immense.

A weekly blog on your website that you also feed to Facebook and link to on Twitter provides a great way to connect with your potential and current customers in a personal and informative way.

Best of all, it keeps you at the forefront of their mind, and if you strike the right tone and create interest, it can build your reputation as the authority in your industry.

Be Social

Social media is increasingly the tool that businesses use to reach out directly to their customers.

Whether it's a quick marketing email or using your business Facebook page to actively engage with patrons and seek feedback, social media savvy is a must.

It's also imperative businesses not only establish their social media presence but maintain and monitor it, answering queries, dealing with negative feedback, and ensuring profiles and details are up to date across the board, including professional profiles like LinkedIn.

Business owners should be checking into social media regularly or allocating it as a task to staff members.

Maintain your Websites

These days, business is as much about an internet presence as it is a physical location, so ensure your website is professional, easy to understand and relevant.

Your website should be updated at least once a year to ensure the style is contemporary and reflects your growing enterprise including any branding changes.

That's not to mention those blogs we talked about before.

Prepare in Advance

When devising media strategies that embrace the traditional industries like print, radio and television, prepare them in advance.

If you know you're launching a product or celebrating a milestone, have your media release drafted long before the event so you control the distribution and have the details locked in to maximise its potential.

Maintaining your media presence is an ongoing process that takes time and effort each week.

By planning for it, factoring it in and setting aside time for tasks, you maximise the potential of your message being heard.

My Final Tips

Keep telling Your Story

Make sure you keep telling your story. It is not possible for a journalist to read every release they are sent.

Think like a Journalist

Think like a journalist when writing and submitting your ideas. Ask yourself "why would someone want to read this?".

Ask for Help

The world of PR and marketing can be very confusing. Ask for help to make your way. PR coaches, agencies and mentors are all there to support and guide you.

More Reading and Resources

PR Sites and Resources

SourceBottle: SourceBottle has great leads for reverse pitching to the media. **sourcebottle.com**

MediaScope: MediaScope offers a growing range of resources and services for marketers, agencies, media owners, advertising sales specialists, and everyone involved in the media trading process. **mediascope.com.au**

Courses

How to Write a Media Release

Take a tour with Ideas and Marketing strategist Linda Reed-Enever of the ins and outs of how to write a Media Release.

How to Create an Available for Interview Profile to Pitch to the Media

An "Available for Interview" Profile allows you to showcase your expertise and business to the media. Its purpose is to put you forward as a talent the media can call on when it comes to topics and issues affecting your industry.

The P's of Podcasting

Join Ideas Strategist Linda Reed-Enever, as she shares the processes, procedures and protocols of podcasting, drawing on the planning, tools and platforms she and the Enever Group Team use when creating podcasts both in-house and with clients.

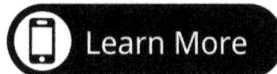

Learn More

Tools

Grammarly provides real-time suggestions to improve your team's writing instantly. It is the ultimate "writing assistant" that writers, course creators, and other professionals can use to proofread and edit their documents. **snip.ly/grammarly**

Canva makes design fun, simple, and easy. They have opened up design to the average user with great tools, easy-to-follow templates, and customising tools. The more you use it, the more creative you will become. **snip.ly/canva30pro**

ChatGPT is a large language model chatbot developed by OpenAI. It has a remarkable ability to interact in conversational dialogue form and provide responses that can appear surprisingly human. **snip.ly/chatgpteg**

Pepper Content is a copywriting tool powered by artificial intelligence that helps you write better, and faster. It's like having your own personal content-writing assistant! **snip.ly/peppercontent**

Rytr is an AI writing assistant that helps you create high-quality content, in just a few seconds, at a fraction of the cost! Generate killer content, effortlessly from blogs to emails to ad copies, and auto-generate catchy, original, and high-converting copies in popular tones & languages in just a few seconds. Just pick a use case, enter some context, and boom...your copy is ready! **snip.ly/rytr**

Headline Analyzer by CoSchedule is a free blog post headline analyzer will score your overall headline quality and rate its ability to result in social shares, increased traffic, and SEO value. It works well for both blogs and releases too. **snip.ly/coschedule**

The Emotional Headline Analyzer is a handy tool to run your headlines because emotion has a lot to do with why people read beyond a headline or click on it in the first place. **snip.ly/aminstitute**

About Linda Reed-Enever

With more than 20 years of expertise in marketing and public relations, Linda Reed-Enever specialises in assisting business owners tell their story.

Renowned as the PR & Marketing Ideas Strategist, she successfully created ThoughtSpot PR (Now Enever Group) in 2012.

In a bid to further assist operators navigating the challenging small business landscape, she launched the online community BusinessBusinessBusiness in 2014 where she offers her PR and marketing expertise to a community of more than 30,000.

In addition, Linda is renowned as public relations educator and strategist, supporting business through courses that offer the tools and insight they need to connect with the media and hone their brand.

You can find further tips and insight from Linda at
enevergroup.com.au.